THE NATURE NOTEBOOK SERIES

———————————————

THE TREE NOTEBOOK

EDITED BY

ANNA BOTSFORD COMSTOCK

——————————————————

THE COMSTOCK PUBLISHING COMPANY
ITHACA, NEW YORK

THIS EDITION PUBLISHED 2021
BY LIVING BOOK PRESS IN ASSOCIATION WITH
HEARTHROOM PRESS

ILLUSTRATIONS BY: W.C. BAKER & ANNA C. STRYKE

ORIGINAL WORK PUBLISHED
IN 1914
BY
COMSTOCK PUBLISHING
COMPANY

A SPECIAL THANKS TO

THE MORTON ARBORETUM

FOR THEIR WORK IN PRESERVATION AND
FOR THE KINDNESS AND GENEROSITY
OFFERED THE PUBLISHER IN THE
RESEARCH OF THIS BOOK.

FOR MORE INFORMATION, CONTACT:
HEARTHROOM PRESS
INFO@HEARTHROOMPRESS.COM

ISBN: 978-1-922634-38-2

A catalogue record for this
book is available from the
NATIONAL
LIBRARY   National Library of Australia
OF AUSTRALIA

INDEX TO TREE NOTES

Name of tree   Page

....

....

....

....

....

....

....

....

....

....

....

....

....

....

....

....

....

....

....

....

....

....

....

....

....

....

....

....

....

....

....

....

....

....

....

INDEX TO TREE NOTES

NAME OF TREE   PAGE

he work of this notebook should combine schoolroom study with field observation. The first three pages of notes on each piece should be answered and completed in the field with the tree under direct observation. The commercial use of the tree and other interesting facts about the species may be written on the fourth page after consulting books on trees and forestry.

The pictures of leaves given in the first part are not intended to take the place of a tree book for identification of species. They are given simply as an aid in determining the trees when in the field, so as to render it unnecessary to carry the tree book while taking the notes. Leaves, blossoms, or fruit from the trees should be carried to the school-room or home for careful drawing. Care should be taken to label these by numbers as soon as collected so that there will be no mistake in the notes. Unless the observer is expert in drawing, it would be better to trace the leaves on the notebook page so as to be sure of absolute accuracy.

The questions in the notebook are planned so that many of them may be answered by underscoring the word which describes the particular tree that is being studied. A fairly large tree should be chosen for study; this notebook is not planned to include shrubs.

The fourth page should be a summary of all that is known about the tree, as to its lumber or other uses made of it by man, and any historical facts of interest concerning the species. Encyclopedias may be consulted for this as well as the various manuals of trees and forestry. Allusions to the tree in literature should also be included.

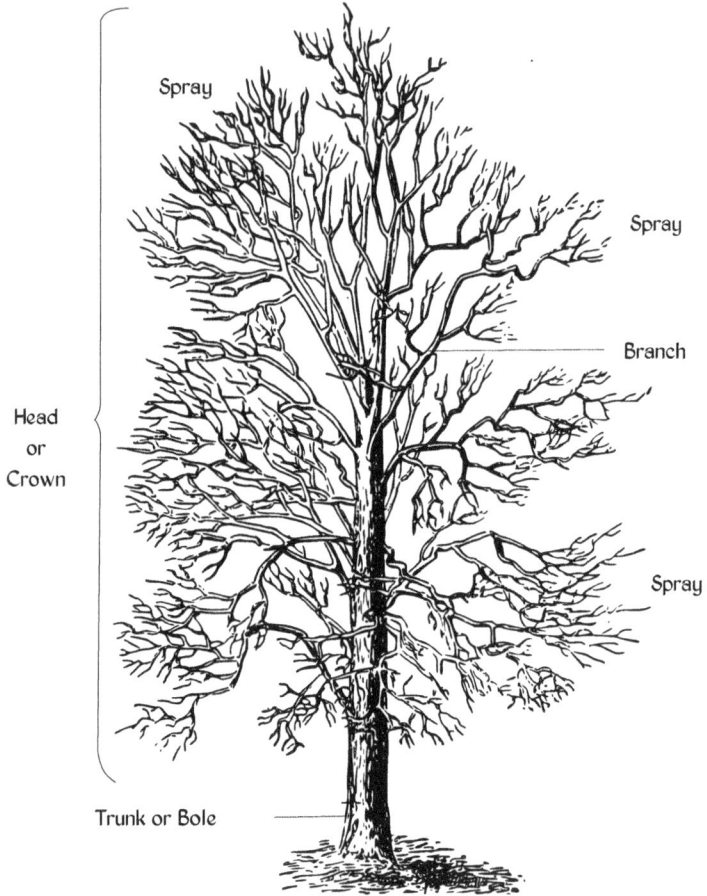

Spray

Spray

Branch

Head
or
Crown

Spray

Trunk or Bole

A Tree with Parts Named

Perhaps the easiest way to to guess at the height of a tree is to take a stick five feet long, set it up against the trunk of the tree then step back for a distance and estimate how many lengths of this stick would be required to reach the top-most branches of the tree. A tape measure may be carried in the pocket and the stick measured with this, which will mae it unnecessary to be burdened by a stick while tramping about.

The following is another method of measuring a tree which stands in the open: Choose a bright, sunny morning or afternoon. Place your stick in the ground by the side of the tree so that five feet will project above the soil. Then with a tape measure get the length of the shadow of the tree and the length of the shadow of the stick. If the shadow of the stick is six feet long and the shadow of the tree is 90 feet long, then your example will be 6ft.: 5ft.::90ft.: ? The tree would be 75 feet high.

To measure the circumference of the tree find the exact measurement four feet from the ground. To find the diameter of the trunk divide the circumference by 3.15.

Other and more scientific methods of measuring trees are giving in First Book of Forestry, Roth, p. 171, and in New England Trees in Winter, Blakeslee & Jarvis, pp. 313-317 in the introduction.

Map showing the tree regions of the united states and Canada.

Mark upon it a red X to show where you live. This will help you keep in mind the types of trees you expect to find.

8

HOW TO USE THE FOLLOWING PAGES TO IDENTIFY LEAVES

Note the size of the leaf as given and look at the scale below to fix the size in your mind.

Note whether the tree grows in your region as shown on the map on the opposite page.

Note whether the leaves are opposite or alternate. The maples, the ashes and buckeyes and horse-chestnut are the only common trees that have leaves placed opposite.

Scarlet Oak 3-6" , I, II, N.IV, M.V. Means "The scarlet oak has leaves three to six inches long and is found in regions I, II and Middle V as shown on the map.

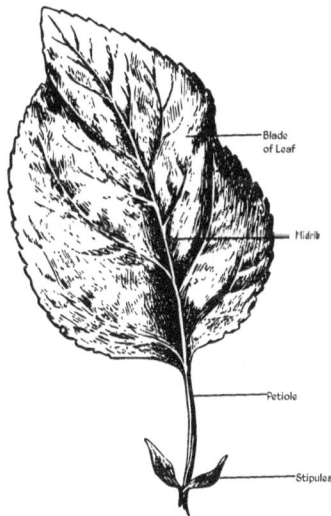

A leaf with parts named

Simple Leaves

Compound Leaves

Simple Leaves

Placed opposite

Simple Leaves

Placed alternate

Compound Leaves

Placed opposite

Compound Leaves

Placed alternate

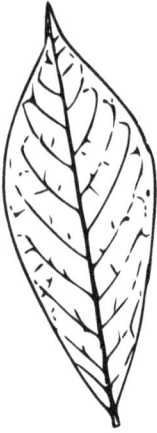

Pawpaw
8-12". I, III, V, VI.
Often a shrub

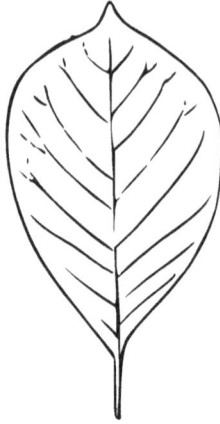

*Tupelo, Pepperidge
Or Sour Gum*
2-5". I, II, III, IV, V.

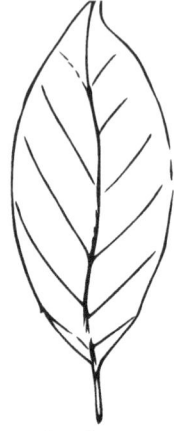

Persimmon
3-7". II, III, IV, V.

*Judas Tree or
Redbud*
3-5". I, II, IV, V.

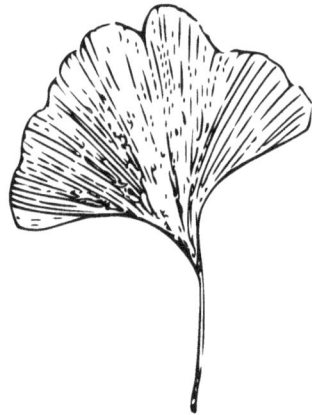

Ghinko
Ornamental.
Introduced from
China and Japan.

Swamp Magnolia or
Sweet Bay 4-6". II, III,
S.IV.

Cucumber Tree or
Mountain Magnolia
7-10". I, III, IV.

Umbrella Tree
12-18". II and S.IV.

Tulip, Whitewood
or
Yellow Poplar
5-6". I, II, III, IV.

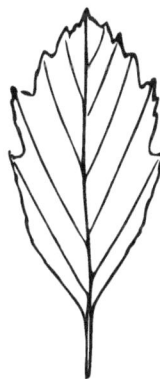

Dotted Haw or
Thornapple
2-3". S.I, II, IV.

THE POPLARS

There are seven common native poplars. The Swamp poplar of the South is not figured here.

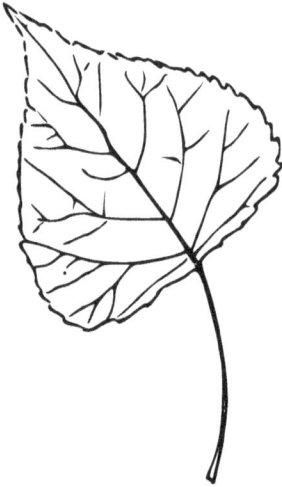

Cottonwood or Carolina Poplar
3-7". I, II, III, IV, V, VI, VII. There is in VI and VII also a narrow leaf cottonwood.

Quaking Aspen or Aspen
1.5-3". I, N.IV, N.V, VI, VII.

White Silver-lead Poplar or Abele
3-4". Lower side of leaf white cottony. Introduced from Europe.

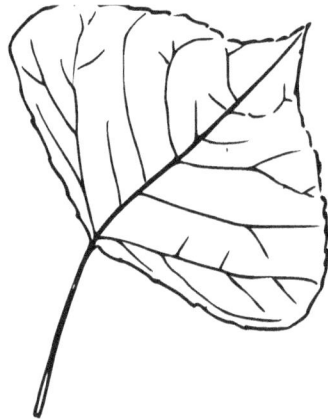

Lombardy Poplar
1-3". Introduced from Europe and Asia.

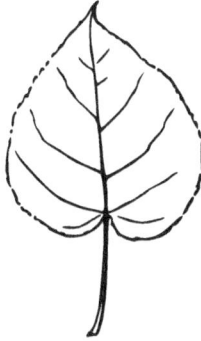

Large Tooth Poplar	Balm of Gilead	Balsam Poplar or Tacmahac
3-6". I, II, IV.	3-6". N.I, IV.	3-6". I, N.IV, N.V, N.VI, N.VII.

THE WILLOWS

There are many species of willows in the United States which are difficult to distinguish by their leaves and so only a few are given.

Peach Leaf Willow	Long Leaf or Sand Bar Willow	Glaucous or Pussy Willow	Yellow Willow Or Golden Osier	Black Willow
2-6". IV, V, VI, VII.	2-6". I,II, IV, V,VI,VII. River Banks	2-5". I, N.II, N.III,N.IV, N.V. Small tree or shrub	2-5". Bright Yellow Branches. Introduced from Europe and naturalized.	3-6". Leaves shining Yellow-green above. I, II, III, IV, V, S.VI. Often several crooked trunks arising from the same base.

THE BIRCHES

There are five native birches which are easily recognized by leaves and bark.

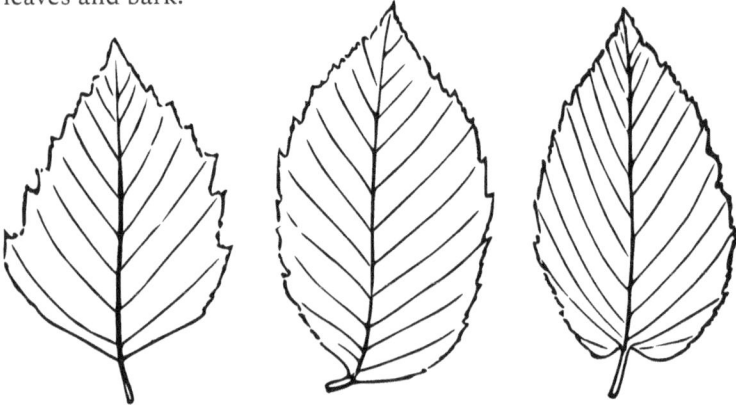

Water, River, or Red Birch
2-14". I, II, III, IV, V. Bark reddish-brown on young trees and separating into scales which curl up making a mat on the trunks of old trees. Small twigs are hairy.

Yellow or Gray Birch
2-5". I, II Bark smooth, shining like satin; yellowish or silver gray, rolling back into ribbon-like stripe. Bark and twigs have a slight wintergreen flavor.

Black or Sweet Birch
2.5-6". I, II, IV. Bark black, often splitting up and down and resembling the bark of Black Cherry. The twigs and leaves taste strongly like wintergreen.

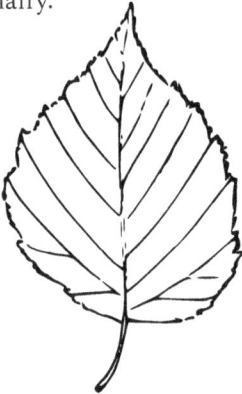

Canoe or Paper Birch
2-4". I, N.V, N.VI, N. VII. Bark creamy white and beneath outer layer the bark separates into paper-like layers.

White, Gray, or Old Field Birch
2.5-3.5". A small tree; bark dull creamy white with dark triangular marks. Leaves quiver like the aspen.

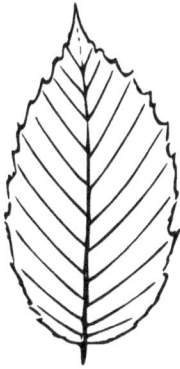

Hop Hornbeam or Ironwood

3-5". I, II, III, IV. Bark grayish, broken into small scales, the fruit resembling that of the hop.

Hornbeam or Blue Beech

2-4". I, II, III, IV, V. Bark fine, bluish-gray, very close fitting over the trunk, which is rigid as if it has muscles underneath.

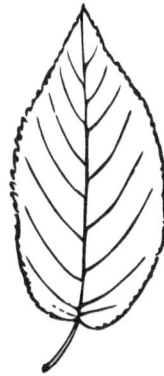

Shadbush Service Tree, or Juneberry

2-4". I, II, IV, VI. Covered with white flowers in early spring.

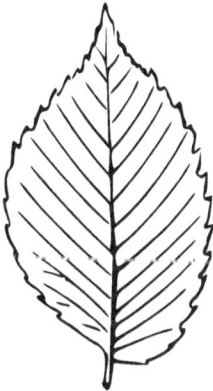

White or American Elm

4-6". I, II, III, IV, V, VI.

Leaves always un-even at base. The slippery or Red Elm has larger leaves which are rough when rubbed in any direction. Inner bark is mucilaginous. The growths along the sides of the twigs and the winged elm of Wahoo has twigs with corky wings. The English Elms planted in parks have fruit much larger than the American.

Chestnut

6-9". I, II, IV. Distinguished from Chestnut Oak by the sharp teeth on the margin of the leaves.

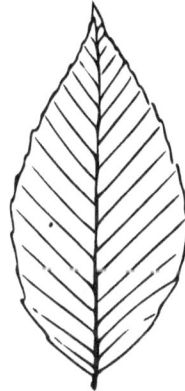

Beech

3-6". I, II, III, IV. Smooth, close fitting, grayish-blue bark; buds slender and sharp pointed.

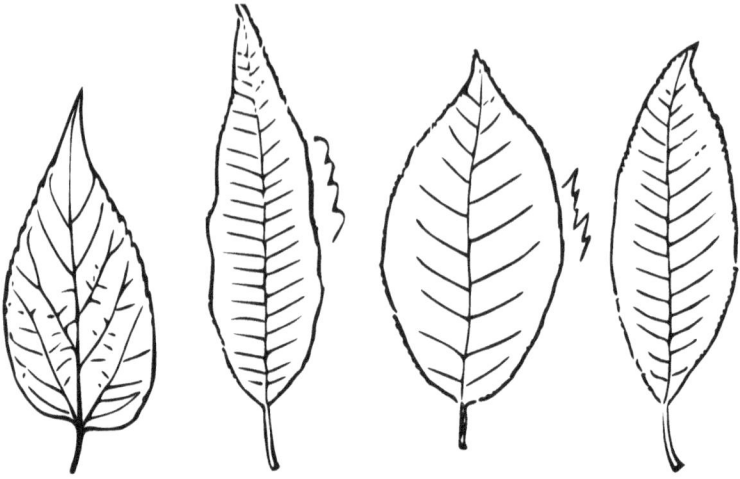

Hackberry, Sugarberry or Nettle Tree 2.5-4". I, II, III, IV, V, VI, VII. Veins of leaves very prominent.

Wild, Bird Pigeon, Pin, Red Cherry 3-5". I, II, N.V, N.VI, N.VII. Fruit red.

Choke Cherry 2-4". I, II, III, IV, V, VI, V, VI. Fruit red and astringent.

Wild Black Cherry 2-5". I, II, III, IV, V, VI, V. Fruit black.

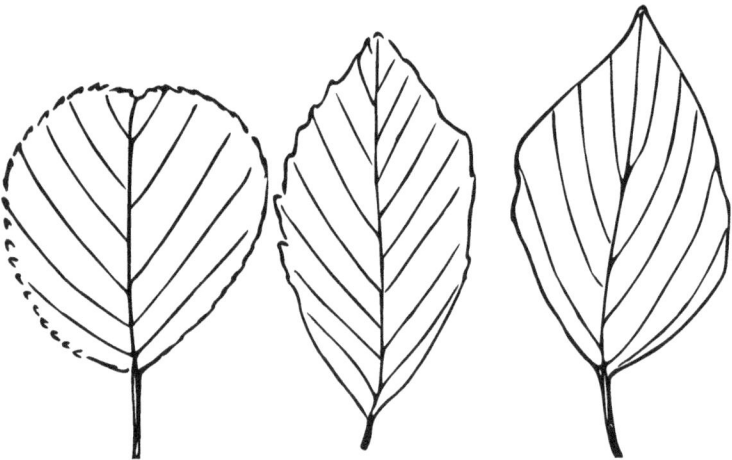

Black Alder 2-5". Small tree introduced from Europe.

Speckled Alder 2-5". Small tree near streams.

Flowering Dogwood 2-5". S.I, II, III, IV, V.

Sweet or Red Gum,
Liquid-amber
3-5". II, III, IV.

Mulberry
3-5". S.I, III, IV, V.
Leaves often lobed
like a mitten

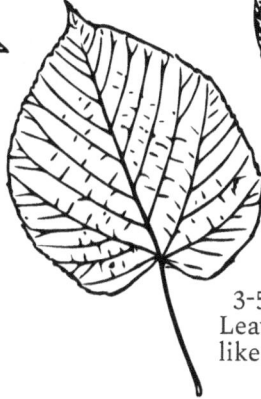

Basswood or American
Linden
5-10". I, II, IV, V, E.V.

Sycamore or Buttonwood
4-9". I, II, III, IV, V.
The base of the leaf stem
is hollow and covers a
bud.

Cut Leaf Maple
4-9". I, II, III, IV, V.
Ornamental. Introduced
from Japan.

THE MAPLES

The eight common native maples and three introduced species may be easily distinguished. The maple leaves are opposite.

Sugar or Rock Maple
3-5". I, II, III, IV, V,
W.VI

Norway Maple
3-5".   Ornamental.
Introduced   from
Norway.

The black Maple is a Sugar Maple variety of II, IV, S.V. It's leaves are three lobed, untoothed, and the bark of the trunk is black.

Silver, Soft or White Maple
5-7". I, II, III, IV, V, W.VI
Leaves silvery white under-neath.

Red, Scarlet, Swamp or Soft Maple
2-6". I, II, III, IV, V.
Margin of the leaves toothed near the petiole.

Ash-leaved Maple or Boxelder
I, II, IV, V, VI.
Leaves compound with three
to five irregular leaflets.

Sycamore Maple
3-5". Ornamental.
Introduced from Europe.

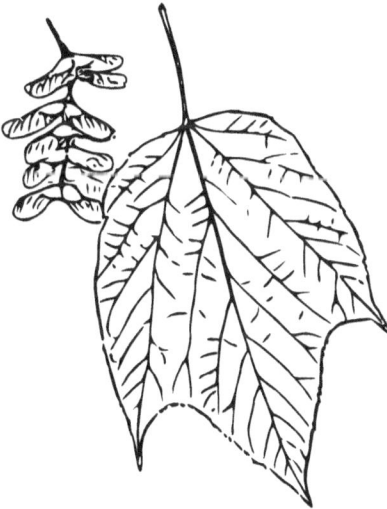

Striped or Goosefoot Maple or
Moosewood
5-6". I, II, N.IV. A small tree or
shrub with greenish or brown
bark, with narrow white stripes
running up and down.

Mountain Maple
4-5". A small tree or shrub in
forests and on banks of
streams.

THE BLACK OAKS

The trees of the Black Oak group have the lobes of leaves tipped with spines. Acorns bitter, requiring two years to ripen; bark dark. The Red, Black, and Pin Oaks often have the leaves on the upper branches similar; the leaves on the lower branches are more typical.

Red Oak
7-9". I, II, IV, N.V.
Acorn large with
shallow cup.

Scarlet Oak
3-6". I, II, N.IV,
M.V.

Pin or Swamp Oak
4-6". I, II, N.IV.

Black or Yellow Oak
5-7". I, II, III, IV, V. Two
types of Black Oak leaves.

Shingle Oak
4-6". II, IV, V.

Spanish Oak
6-7". III, S.IV, S.V.

Water, Duck or
Possum Oak
2-6". III, S.IV.

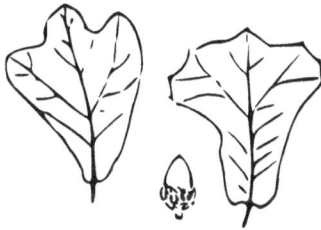

Black Jack
3-8". II, III, IV, V. Grows on
dry sandy soil.

Bear, Barren or Scarlet Oak
2-5". I, E.II. Usually along
coast or sandy barrens.

Willow Oak
2-5". III, S.IV.

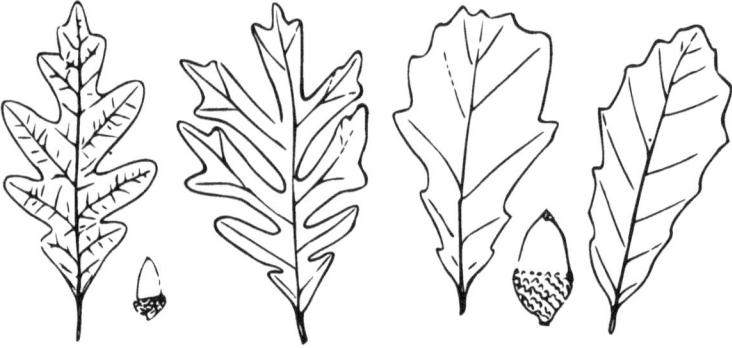

White Oak
5-9". I, II, III, IV, V.

Black or Yellow Oak
5-7". I, II, III, IV, V. Two
types of Black Oak leaves.

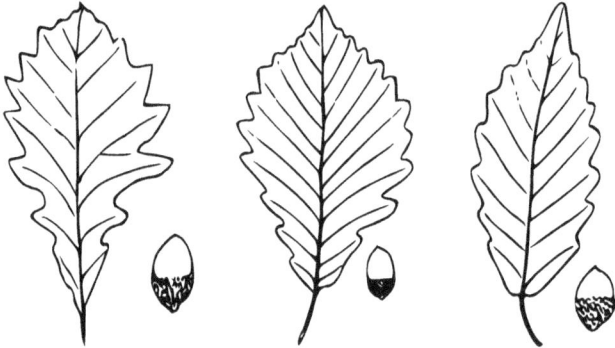

Chestnut or Yellow
Oak
4-7". S.I, II, IV, V.
Leaves are very much
like those of the
Chestnut except the
lobes are more
rounded.

Swamp White Oak
5-6". S.I, II, N.IV,
M.V.

Chestnut, Cow,
Basket Oak
5-9". I, II, III, S.IV,
S.V.

Bur or Mossy Cup Oak
4-8". I, IV, V, VI. Cup of the
acorn fringed.

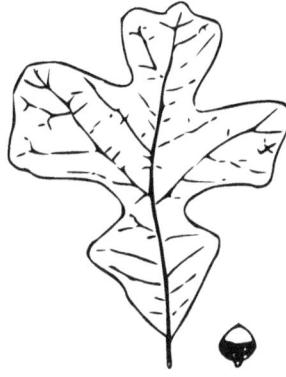

Post Oak
5-8". II, III, IV, V.

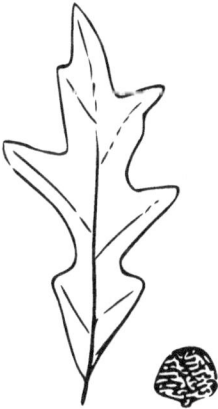

Overcup Oak
4-6". III, S.IV, S.V. Cup
completely covers the acorn.

Live Oak
2-4". III, S.V, S.VI.

THE LOCUSTS

Trees with compound leaves. The fruit, a pod.

Honey Locust
7-8". II, IV, V. Seven to ten pairs of leaflets. Pod 8 to 18" long.

Black or Yellow Locust
8-14". S.I, II. Seven to nine pairs of leaflets. Pod 3 to 4" long.

Kentucky Coffee Tree
2-3". Twice compound. IV, V.

Ailanthus
12-13". Ornamental. Introduced from China and Japan.

Mountain Ash
6-10". Fruit bright scarlet berries in clusters.

THE ASHES

Red Ash. Leaves much like White Ash but petioles are velvety. I, II, III, IV, V.

Green Ash. Leaves like Red Ash, smooth petiole, but leaflets are green beneath. II, IV, V, VI.

Blue Ash. 8-11" IV, V. Twigs with four ridges, making them square in cross section.

The Ashes have compound leaves placed opposite.

White Ash
8-15". Five to eleven leaflets which are light underneath with long stalks; stems smooth. I, II, III, IV, V.

Black or Hoop Ash
8-12". Seven to eleven leaflets not stalked but set directly on the mid stem; stems smooth. I, II, II, N.V.

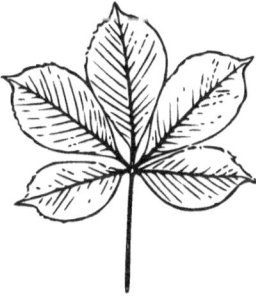

Horse-chestnut
5-7". Ornamental. Introduced from Europe. The Horse-chestnut leaf usually has seven leaflets, while the Ohio and sweet Buckeye have usually but five.

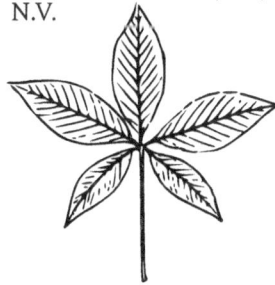

Ohio Buckeye
3-6". Seven Leaves and bark when crushed have disagreeable odor. Fruit husks are prickly; flowers yellowish-green.

Sweet or Yellow Buckeye
4-7". II, IV. Fruit husk smooth; flowers yellow or pink.

THE HICKORIES

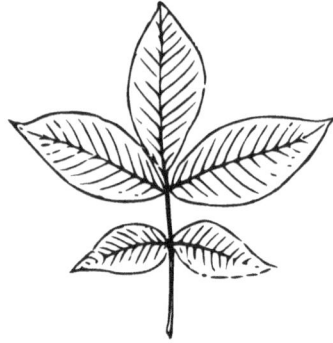

Mockernut or Big Bud
8-15". Usually seven to nine leaflets, I, II, III, IV, S.V. Leaves fragrant when crushed, Outer shell of nut very thick, kernel sweet, terminal buds large. Bark somewhat resembling shagbark but smoother.

Shellbark or Shagbark Hickory
8-10". Five, rarely seven leaflets, I, II, IV, E.VI. Bark scales off in long, loose plates; kernel delicious.

Kingnut or Big Shellbark
12-14". Seven leaflets. II, IV, V. Bark like the shellbark; young branches yellow.

Bitternut
6-10". Seven to eleven leaflets set directly on central stem. I, II, IV, V. E.VI. Nuts often broader than long; husks thin, meat bitter.

Pignut
8-12". Leaflets five, seven or nine. I, II, III, IV, V. E.VI. Fruit pear-shaped. Kernel slightly bitter.

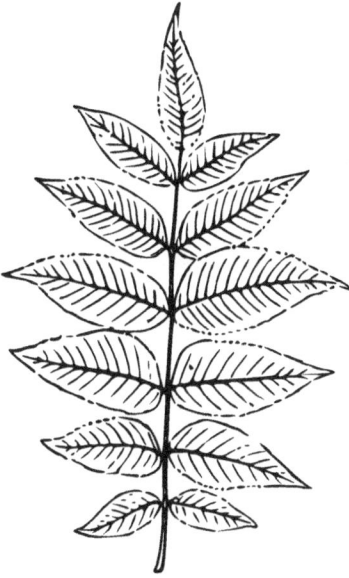

Butternut or White Walnut
11-30". Leaflets 11 to 19. I, II, IV, V. Leaf stalk sticky; nut oblong. Pith of the twigs dark brown.

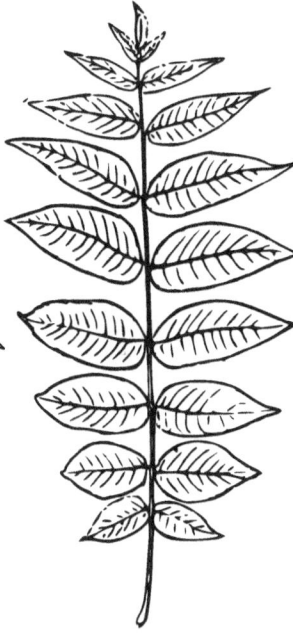

Black Walnut
12-24". Leaflets 13 to 23. I, II, IV, V, E.VI. Leaf stems not sticky; nut round. Pith of the twigs yellow.

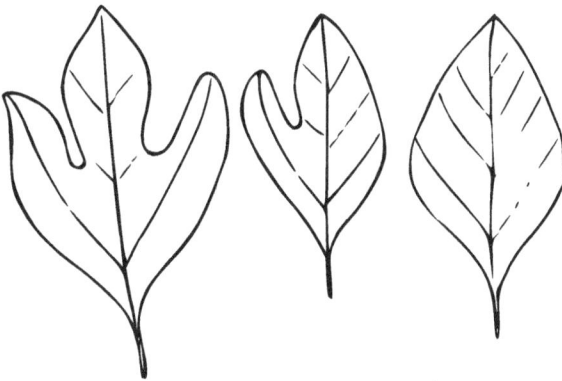

Sassafras. 3-7". I, II, III, IV, V.

NOTES ON TREES

Date ....

Name of tree ....

1. Where is it growing? Hillside, near stream, swamp, mountain, valley, open field, along fences, in the forest, along the edge of the forest

2. If growing in the open, indicate its general shape thus: Select one of the following outlines most closely resembling the tree with the pencil and add the trunk showing its proportion to the head of the tree and draw in the larger branches, changing the outline to represent the tree.

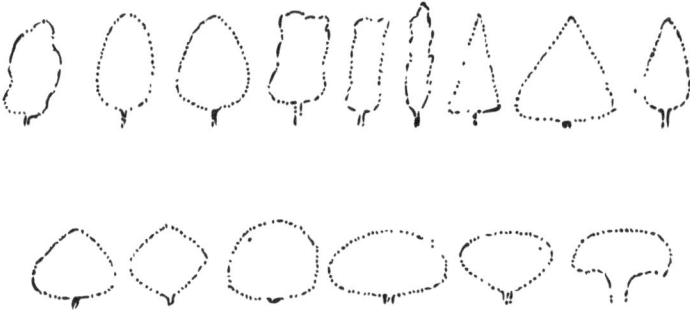

3. Does the bole or trunk extend straight up through the head or does it divide into branches? Are there many small branches or few large branches?

4. Is the bark of tree rough, smooth, scaly, or is it divided by fissures?

5. Do the fissures extend up and down or crosswise or in both directions? Are the ridges between the fissures sharp, rounded, or flattened? How many inches across the ridge from the bottom of the fissure on each side?

6. Are the surface layers of the bark stiff or flexible? Are they fast to the tree or easily peeled off? Are they shed in stripes or in bits?

7. Is the color of the bark white, gray, dark gray, blackish, blotched, yellowish-brown, reddish-brown, or dark brown?

8. Are the leaves placed alternate or opposite on the twigs? Is the leaf simple or compound?

9. Is the leaf polished, smooth, dull, rough, or hairy on the upper side? Compare the upper and undersides in color and texture.

10. Sketch or trace the leaf showing the stem, the petiole, and the veins, and be especially careful to draw the edges accurately.

11. When does the tree blossom?

Are the flowers perfect or are those that bear pollen separate from those that develop the fruit? If so, are they on the same tree or on different trees?

12. Describe or sketch the blossoms of the tree.

13. When is the fruit ripe? Describe it or sketch it and tell how it is carried from the parent tree so that the seeds may find a place to grow.

Consult the manuals of forestry and tree books and give an account of every thing that is of interest concerning this tree, including its native place, its history and its uses by man; and any quotations from literature ---- especially poetry that may have been written concerning this species.

Date ....

Name of tree ....

1. Where is it growing? Hillside, near stream, swamp, mountain, valley, open field, along fences, in the forest, along the edge of the forest

2. If growing in the open, indicate its general shape thus: Select one of the following outlines most closely resembling the tree with the pencil and add the trunk showing its proportion to the head of the tree and draw in the larger branches, changing the outline to represent the tree.

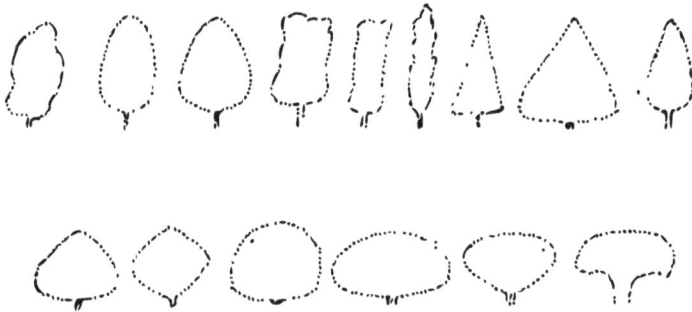

3. Does the bole or trunk extend straight up through the head or does it divide into branches? Are there many small branches or few large branches?

4. Is the bark of tree rough, smooth, scaly, or is it divided by fissures?

5. Do the fissures extend up and down or crosswise or in both directions? Are the ridges between the fissures sharp, rounded, or flattened? How many inches across the ridge from the bottom of the fissure on each side?

6. Are the surface layers of the bark stiff or flexible? Are they fast to the tree or easily peeled off? Are they shed in stripes or in bits?

7. Is the color of the bark white, gray, dark gray, blackish, blotched, yellowish-brown, reddish-brown, or dark brown?

8. Are the leaves placed alternate or opposite on the twigs? Is the leaf simple or compound?

9. Is the leaf polished, smooth, dull, rough, or hairy on the upper side? Compare the upper and undersides in color and texture.

10. Sketch or trace the leaf showing the stem, the petiole, and the veins, and be especially careful to draw the edges accurately.

11. When does the tree blossom?

Are the flowers perfect or are those that bear pollen separate from those that develop the fruit? If so, are they on the same tree or on different trees?

12. Describe or sketch the blossoms of the tree.

13. When is the fruit ripe? Describe it or sketch it and tell how it is carried from the parent tree so that the seeds may find a place to grow.

Consult the manuals of forestry and tree books and give an account of every thing that is of interest concerning this tree, including its native place, its history and its uses by man; and any quotations from literature ---- especially poetry that may have been written concerning this species.

Date ....

Name of tree ....

1. Where is it growing? Hillside, near stream, swamp, mountain, valley, open field, along fences, in the forest, along the edge of the forest

2. If growing in the open, indicate its general shape thus: Select one of the following outlines most closely resembling the tree with the pencil and add the trunk showing its proportion to the head of the tree and draw in the larger branches, changing the outline to represent the tree.

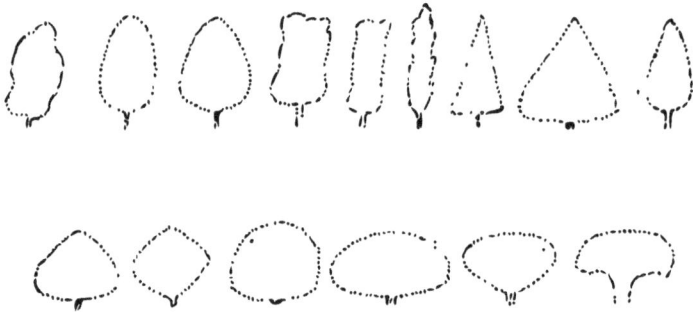

3. Does the bole or trunk extend straight up through the head or does it divide into branches? Are there many small branches or few large branches?

4. Is the bark of tree rough, smooth, scaly, or is it divided by fissures?

5. Do the fissures extend up and down or crosswise or in both directions? Are the ridges between the fissures sharp, rounded, or flattened? How many inches across the ridge from the bottom of the fissure on each side?

6. Are the surface layers of the bark stiff or flexible? Are they fast to the tree or easily peeled off? Are they shed in stripes or in bits?

7. Is the color of the bark white, gray, dark gray, blackish, blotched, yellowish-brown, reddish-brown, or dark brown?

8. Are the leaves placed alternate or opposite on the twigs? Is the leaf simple or compound?

9. Is the leaf polished, smooth, dull, rough, or hairy on the upper side? Compare the upper and undersides in color and texture.

10. Sketch or trace the leaf showing the stem, the petiole, and the veins, and be especially careful to draw the edges accurately.

11. When does the tree blossom?

Are the flowers perfect or are those that bear pollen separate from those that develop the fruit? If so, are they on the same tree or on different trees?

12. Describe or sketch the blossoms of the tree.

13. When is the fruit ripe? Describe it or sketch it and tell how it is carried from the parent tree so that the seeds may find a place to grow.

Consult the manuals of forestry and tree books and give an account of every thing that is of interest concerning this tree, including its native place, its history and its uses by man; and any quotations from literature ---- especially poetry that may have been written concerning this species.

Date ....

Name of tree ....

1. Where is it growing? Hillside, near stream, swamp, mountain, valley, open field, along fences, in the forest, along the edge of the forest

2. If growing in the open, indicate its general shape thus: Select one of the following outlines most closely resembling the tree with the pencil and add the trunk showing its proportion to the head of the tree and draw in the larger branches, changing the outline to represent the tree.

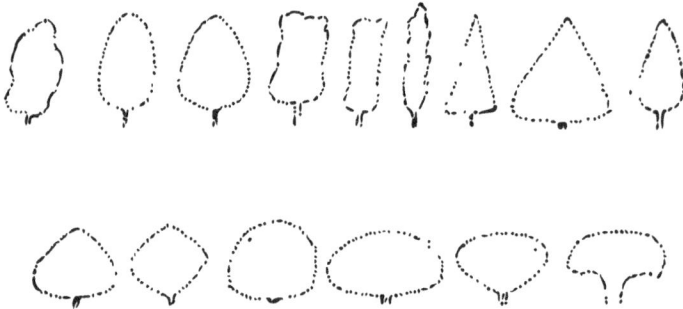

3. Does the bole or trunk extend straight up through the head or does it divide into branches? Are there many small branches or few large branches?

4. Is the bark of tree rough, smooth, scaly, or is it divided by fissures?

5. Do the fissures extend up and down or crosswise or in both directions? Are the ridges between the fissures sharp, rounded, or flattened? How many inches across the ridge from the bottom of the fissure on each side?

6. Are the surface layers of the bark stiff or flexible? Are they fast to the tree or easily peeled off? Are they shed in stripes or in bits?

7. Is the color of the bark white, gray, dark gray, blackish, blotched, yellowish-brown, reddish-brown, or dark brown?

8. Are the leaves placed alternate or opposite on the twigs? Is the leaf simple or compound?

9. Is the leaf polished, smooth, dull, rough, or hairy on the upper side? Compare the upper and undersides in color and texture.

10. Sketch or trace the leaf showing the stem, the petiole, and the veins, and be especially careful to draw the edges accurately.

11. When does the tree blossom?

Are the flowers perfect or are those that bear pollen separate from those that develop the fruit? If so, are they on the same tree or on different trees?

12. Describe or sketch the blossoms of the tree.

13. When is the fruit ripe? Describe it or sketch it and tell how it is carried from the parent tree so that the seeds may find a place to grow.

Consult the manuals of forestry and tree books and give an account of every thing that is of interest concerning this tree, including its native place, its history and its uses by man; and any quotations from literature ---- especially poetry that may have been written concerning this species.

Date ....

Name of tree ....

1. Where is it growing? Hillside, near stream, swamp, mountain, valley, open field, along fences, in the forest, along the edge of the forest

2. If growing in the open, indicate its general shape thus: Select one of the following outlines most closely resembling the tree with the pencil and add the trunk showing its proportion to the head of the tree and draw in the larger branches, changing the outline to represent the tree.

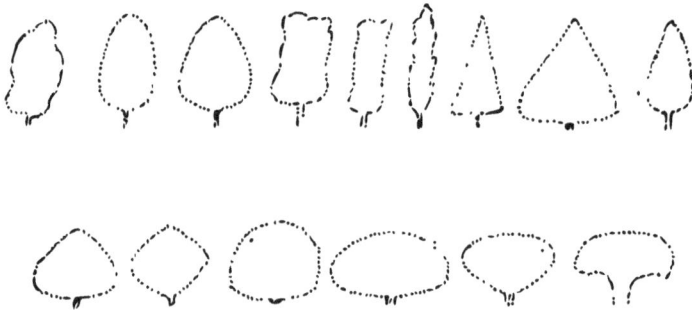

3. Does the bole or trunk extend straight up through the head or does it divide into branches? Are there many small branches or few large branches?

4. Is the bark of tree rough, smooth, scaly, or is it divided by fissures?

5. Do the fissures extend up and down or crosswise or in both directions? Are the ridges between the fissures sharp, rounded, or flattened? How many inches across the ridge from the bottom of the fissure on each side?

6. Are the surface layers of the bark stiff or flexible? Are they fast to the tree or easily peeled off? Are they shed in stripes or in bits?

7. Is the color of the bark white, gray, dark gray, blackish, blotched, yellowish-brown, reddish-brown, or dark brown?

8. Are the leaves placed alternate or opposite on the twigs? Is the leaf simple or compound?

9. Is the leaf polished, smooth, dull, rough, or hairy on the upper side? Compare the upper and undersides in color and texture.

10. Sketch or trace the leaf showing the stem, the petiole, and the veins, and be especially careful to draw the edges accurately.

11. When does the tree blossom?

Are the flowers perfect or are those that bear pollen separate from those that develop the fruit? If so, are they on the same tree or on different trees?

12. Describe or sketch the blossoms of the tree.

13. When is the fruit ripe? Describe it or sketch it and tell how it is carried from the parent tree so that the seeds may find a place to grow.

Consult the manuals of forestry and tree books and give an account of every thing that is of interest concerning this tree, including its native place, its history and its uses by man; and any quotations from literature ---- especially poetry that may have been written concerning this species.

Underscore the Words Which Describe the Tree

Date ....

Name of tree ....

1. Where is it growing? Hillside, near stream, swamp, mountain, valley, open field, along fences, in the forest, along the edge of the forest

2. If growing in the open, indicate its general shape thus: Select one of the following outlines most closely resembling the tree with the pencil and add the trunk showing its proportion to the head of the tree and draw in the larger branches, changing the outline to represent the tree.

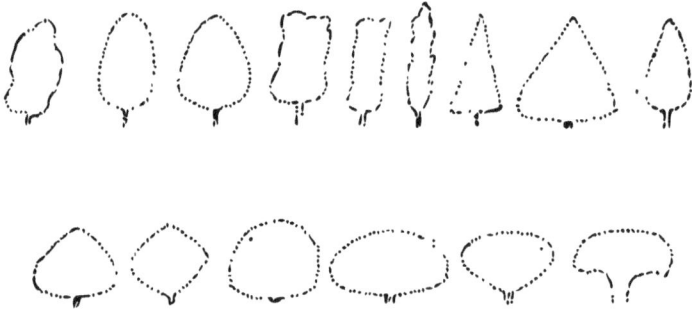

3. Does the bole or trunk extend straight up through the head or does it divide into branches? Are there many small branches or few large branches?

4. Is the bark of tree rough, smooth, scaly, or is it divided by fissures?

5. Do the fissures extend up and down or crosswise or in both directions? Are the ridges between the fissures sharp, rounded, or flattened? How many inches across the ridge from the bottom of the fissure on each side?

6. Are the surface layers of the bark stiff or flexible? Are they fast to the tree or easily peeled off? Are they shed in stripes or in bits?

7. Is the color of the bark white, gray, dark gray, blackish, blotched, yellowish-brown, reddish-brown, or dark brown?

8. Are the leaves placed alternate or opposite on the twigs? Is the leaf simple or compound?

9. Is the leaf polished, smooth, dull, rough, or hairy on the upper side? Compare the upper and undersides in color and texture.

10. Sketch or trace the leaf showing the stem, the petiole, and the veins, and be especially careful to draw the edges accurately.

11. When does the tree blossom?

Are the flowers perfect or are those that bear pollen separate from those that develop the fruit? If so, are they on the same tree or on different trees?

12. Describe or sketch the blossoms of the tree.

13. When is the fruit ripe? Describe it or sketch it and tell how it is carried from the parent tree so that the seeds may find a place to grow.

Consult the manuals of forestry and tree books and give an account of every thing that is of interest concerning this tree, including its native place, its history and its uses by man; and any quotations from literature ---- especially poetry that may have been written concerning this species.

Date ....

Name of tree ....

1. Where is it growing? Hillside, near stream, swamp, mountain, valley, open field, along fences, in the forest, along the edge of the forest

2. If growing in the open, indicate its general shape thus: Select one of the following outlines most closely resembling the tree with the pencil and add the trunk showing its proportion to the head of the tree and draw in the larger branches, changing the outline to represent the tree.

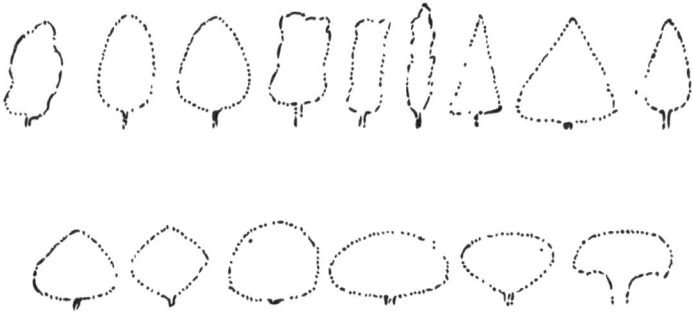

3. Does the bole or trunk extend straight up through the head or does it divide into branches? Are there many small branches or few large branches?

4. Is the bark of tree rough, smooth, scaly, or is it divided by fissures?

5. Do the fissures extend up and down or crosswise or in both directions? Are the ridges between the fissures sharp, rounded, or flattened? How many inches across the ridge from the bottom of the fissure on each side?

6. Are the surface layers of the bark stiff or flexible? Are they fast to the tree or easily peeled off? Are they shed in stripes or in bits?

7. Is the color of the bark white, gray, dark gray, blackish, blotched, yellowish-brown, reddish-brown, or dark brown?

8. Are the leaves placed alternate or opposite on the twigs? Is the leaf simple or compound?

9. Is the leaf polished, smooth, dull, rough, or hairy on the upper side? Compare the upper and undersides in color and texture.

10. Sketch or trace the leaf showing the stem, the petiole, and the veins, and be especially careful to draw the edges accurately.

11. When does the tree blossom?

Are the flowers perfect or are those that bear pollen separate from those that develop the fruit? If so, are they on the same tree or on different trees?

12. Describe or sketch the blossoms of the tree.

13. When is the fruit ripe? Describe it or sketch it and tell how it is carried from the parent tree so that the seeds may find a place to grow.

Consult the manuals of forestry and tree books and give an account of every thing that is of interest concerning this tree, including its native place, its history and its uses by man; and any quotations from literature ---- especially poetry that may have been written concerning this species.

UNDERSCORE THE WORDS WHICH DESCRIBE THE TREE

Date ....

Name of tree ....

1. Where is it growing? Hillside, near stream, swamp, mountain, valley, open field, along fences, in the forest, along the edge of the forest

2. If growing in the open, indicate its general shape thus: Select one of the following outlines most closely resembling the tree with the pencil and add the trunk showing its proportion to the head of the tree and draw in the larger branches, changing the outline to represent the tree.

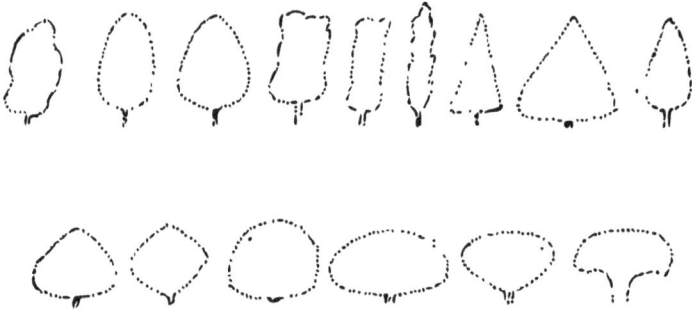

3. Does the bole or trunk extend straight up through the head or does it divide into branches? Are there many small branches or few large branches?

4. Is the bark of tree rough, smooth, scaly, or is it divided by fissures?

5. Do the fissures extend up and down or crosswise or in both directions? Are the ridges between the fissures sharp, rounded, or flattened? How many inches across the ridge from the bottom of the fissure on each side?

6. Are the surface layers of the bark stiff or flexible? Are they fast to the tree or easily peeled off? Are they shed in stripes or in bits?

7. Is the color of the bark white, gray, dark gray, blackish, blotched, yellowish-brown, reddish-brown, or dark brown?

8. Are the leaves placed alternate or opposite on the twigs? Is the leaf simple or compound?

9. Is the leaf polished, smooth, dull, rough, or hairy on the upper side? Compare the upper and undersides in color and texture.

10. Sketch or trace the leaf showing the stem, the petiole, and the veins, and be especially careful to draw the edges accurately.

11. When does the tree blossom?

Are the flowers perfect or are those that bear pollen separate from those that develop the fruit? If so, are they on the same tree or on different trees?

12. Describe or sketch the blossoms of the tree.

13. When is the fruit ripe? Describe it or sketch it and tell how it is carried from the parent tree so that the seeds may find a place to grow.

Consult the manuals of forestry and tree books and give an account of every thing that is of interest concerning this tree, including its native place, its history and its uses by man; and any quotations from literature ---- especially poetry that may have been written concerning this species.

Date ....

Name of tree ....

1. Where is it growing? Hillside, near stream, swamp, mountain, valley, open field, along fences, in the forest, along the edge of the forest

2. If growing in the open, indicate its general shape thus: Select one of the following outlines most closely resembling the tree with the pencil and add the trunk showing its proportion to the head of the tree and draw in the larger branches, changing the outline to represent the tree.

3. Does the bole or trunk extend straight up through the head or does it divide into branches? Are there many small branches or few large branches?

4. Is the bark of tree rough, smooth, scaly, or is it divided by fissures?

5. Do the fissures extend up and down or crosswise or in both directions? Are the ridges between the fissures sharp, rounded, or flattened? How many inches across the ridge from the bottom of the fissure on each side?

6. Are the surface layers of the bark stiff or flexible? Are they fast to the tree or easily peeled off? Are they shed in stripes or in bits?

7. Is the color of the bark white, gray, dark gray, blackish, blotched, yellowish-brown, reddish-brown, or dark brown?

8. Are the leaves placed alternate or opposite on the twigs? Is the leaf simple or compound?

9. Is the leaf polished, smooth, dull, rough, or hairy on the upper side? Compare the upper and undersides in color and texture.

10. Sketch or trace the leaf showing the stem, the petiole, and the veins, and be especially careful to draw the edges accurately.

11. When does the tree blossom?

Are the flowers perfect or are those that bear pollen separate from those that develop the fruit? If so, are they on the same tree or on different trees?

12. Describe or sketch the blossoms of the tree.

13. When is the fruit ripe? Describe it or sketch it and tell how it is carried from the parent tree so that the seeds may find a place to grow.

Consult the manuals of forestry and tree books and give an account of every thing that is of interest concerning this tree, including its native place, its history and its uses by man; and any quotations from literature ---- especially poetry that may have been written concerning this species.

UNDERSCORE THE WORDS WHICH DESCRIBE THE TREE

Date ....

Name of tree ....

1. Where is it growing? Hillside, near stream, swamp, mountain, valley, open field, along fences, in the forest, along the edge of the forest

2. If growing in the open, indicate its general shape thus: Select one of the following outlines most closely resembling the tree with the pencil and add the trunk showing its proportion to the head of the tree and draw in the larger branches, changing the outline to represent the tree.

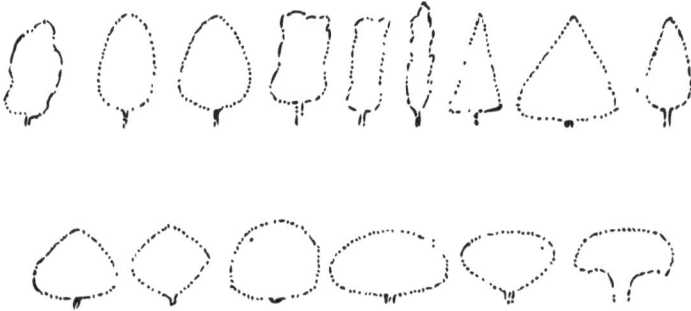

3. Does the bole or trunk extend straight up through the head or does it divide into branches? Are there many small branches or few large branches?

4. Is the bark of tree rough, smooth, scaly, or is it divided by fissures?

5. Do the fissures extend up and down or crosswise or in both directions? Are the ridges between the fissures sharp, rounded, or flattened? How many inches across the ridge from the bottom of the fissure on each side?

6. Are the surface layers of the bark stiff or flexible? Are they fast to the tree or easily peeled off? Are they shed in stripes or in bits?

7. Is the color of the bark white, gray, dark gray, blackish, blotched, yellowish-brown, reddish-brown, or dark brown?

8. Are the leaves placed alternate or opposite on the twigs? Is the leaf simple or compound?

9. Is the leaf polished, smooth, dull, rough, or hairy on the upper side? Compare the upper and undersides in color and texture.

10. Sketch or trace the leaf showing the stem, the petiole, and the veins, and be especially careful to draw the edges accurately.

11. When does the tree blossom?

Are the flowers perfect or are those that bear pollen separate from those that develop the fruit? If so, are they on the same tree or on different trees?

12. Describe or sketch the blossoms of the tree.

13. When is the fruit ripe? Describe it or sketch it and tell how it is carried from the parent tree so that the seeds may find a place to grow.

Consult the manuals of forestry and tree books and give an account of every thing that is of interest concerning this tree, including its native place, its history and its uses by man; and any quotations from literature ---- especially poetry that may have been written concerning this species.

Date ....

Name of tree ....

1. Where is it growing? Hillside, near stream, swamp, mountain, valley, open field, along fences, in the forest, along the edge of the forest

2. If growing in the open, indicate its general shape thus: Select one of the following outlines most closely resembling the tree with the pencil and add the trunk showing its proportion to the head of the tree and draw in the larger branches, changing the outline to represent the tree.

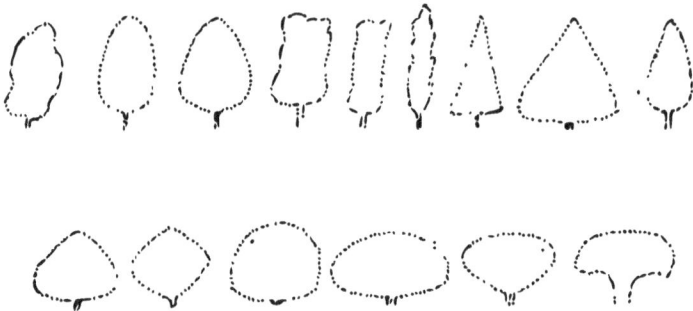

3. Does the bole or trunk extend straight up through the head or does it divide into branches? Are there many small branches or few large branches?

4. Is the bark of tree rough, smooth, scaly, or is it divided by fissures?

5. Do the fissures extend up and down or crosswise or in both directions? Are the ridges between the fissures sharp, rounded, or flattened? How many inches across the ridge from the bottom of the fissure on each side?

6. Are the surface layers of the bark stiff or flexible? Are they fast to the tree or easily peeled off? Are they shed in stripes or in bits?

7. Is the color of the bark white, gray, dark gray, blackish, blotched, yellowish-brown, reddish-brown, or dark brown?

8. Are the leaves placed alternate or opposite on the twigs? Is the leaf simple or compound?

9. Is the leaf polished, smooth, dull, rough, or hairy on the upper side? Compare the upper and undersides in color and texture.

10. Sketch or trace the leaf showing the stem, the petiole, and the veins, and be especially careful to draw the edges accurately.

11. When does the tree blossom?

Are the flowers perfect or are those that bear pollen separate from those that develop the fruit? If so, are they on the same tree or on different trees?

12. Describe or sketch the blossoms of the tree.

13. When is the fruit ripe? Describe it or sketch it and tell how it is carried from the parent tree so that the seeds may find a place to grow.

Consult the manuals of forestry and tree books and give an account of every thing that is of interest concerning this tree, including its native place, its history and its uses by man; and any quotations from literature ---- especially poetry that may have been written concerning this species.

Date ....

Name of tree ....

1. Where is it growing? Hillside, near stream, swamp, mountain, valley, open field, along fences, in the forest, along the edge of the forest

2. If growing in the open, indicate its general shape thus: Select one of the following outlines most closely resembling the tree with the pencil and add the trunk showing its proportion to the head of the tree and draw in the larger branches, changing the outline to represent the tree.

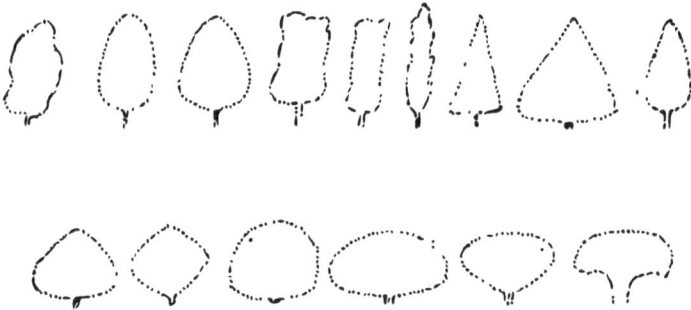

3. Does the bole or trunk extend straight up through the head or does it divide into branches? Are there many small branches or few large branches?

4. Is the bark of tree rough, smooth, scaly, or is it divided by fissures?

5. Do the fissures extend up and down or crosswise or in both directions? Are the ridges between the fissures sharp, rounded, or flattened? How many inches across the ridge from the bottom of the fissure on each side?

6. Are the surface layers of the bark stiff or flexible? Are they fast to the tree or easily peeled off? Are they shed in stripes or in bits?

7. Is the color of the bark white, gray, dark gray, blackish, blotched, yellowish-brown, reddish-brown, or dark brown?

8. Are the leaves placed alternate or opposite on the twigs? Is the leaf simple or compound?

9. Is the leaf polished, smooth, dull, rough, or hairy on the upper side? Compare the upper and undersides in color and texture.

10. Sketch or trace the leaf showing the stem, the petiole, and the veins, and be especially careful to draw the edges accurately.

11. When does the tree blossom?

Are the flowers perfect or are those that bear pollen separate from those that develop the fruit? If so, are they on the same tree or on different trees?

12. Describe or sketch the blossoms of the tree.

13. When is the fruit ripe? Describe it or sketch it and tell how it is carried from the parent tree so that the seeds may find a place to grow.

Consult the manuals of forestry and tree books and give an account of every thing that is of interest concerning this tree, including its native place, its history and its uses by man; and any quotations from literature ---- especially poetry that may have been written concerning this species.

UNDERSCORE THE WORDS WHICH DESCRIBE THE TREE

Date ....

Name of tree ....

1. Where is it growing? Hillside, near stream, swamp, mountain, valley, open field, along fences, in the forest, along the edge of the forest

2. If growing in the open, indicate its general shape thus: Select one of the following outlines most closely resembling the tree with the pencil and add the trunk showing its proportion to the head of the tree and draw in the larger branches, changing the outline to represent the tree.

3. Does the bole or trunk extend straight up through the head or does it divide into branches? Are there many small branches or few large branches?

4. Is the bark of tree rough, smooth, scaly, or is it divided by fissures?

5. Do the fissures extend up and down or crosswise or in both directions? Are the ridges between the fissures sharp, rounded, or flattened? How many inches across the ridge from the bottom of the fissure on each side?

6. Are the surface layers of the bark stiff or flexible? Are they fast to the tree or easily peeled off? Are they shed in stripes or in bits?

7. Is the color of the bark white, gray, dark gray, blackish, blotched, yellowish-brown, reddish-brown, or dark brown?

8. Are the leaves placed alternate or opposite on the twigs? Is the leaf simple or compound?

9. Is the leaf polished, smooth, dull, rough, or hairy on the upper side? Compare the upper and undersides in color and texture.

10. Sketch or trace the leaf showing the stem, the petiole, and the veins, and be especially careful to draw the edges accurately.

11. When does the tree blossom?

Are the flowers perfect or are those that bear pollen separate from those that develop the fruit? If so, are they on the same tree or on different trees?

12. Describe or sketch the blossoms of the tree.

13. When is the fruit ripe? Describe it or sketch it and tell how it is carried from the parent tree so that the seeds may find a place to grow.

Consult the manuals of forestry and tree books and give an account of every thing that is of interest concerning this tree, including its native place, its history and its uses by man; and any quotations from literature ---- especially poetry that may have been written concerning this species.

UNDERSCORE THE WORDS WHICH DESCRIBE THE TREE

Date ....

Name of tree ....

1. Where is it growing? Hillside, near stream, swamp, mountain, valley, open field, along fences, in the forest, along the edge of the forest

2. If growing in the open, indicate its general shape thus: Select one of the following outlines most closely resembling the tree with the pencil and add the trunk showing its proportion to the head of the tree and draw in the larger branches, changing the outline to represent the tree.

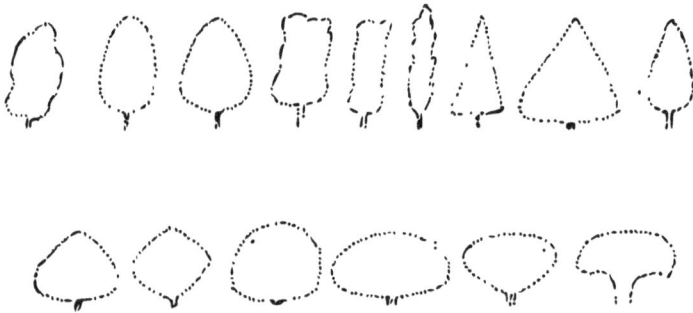

3. Does the bole or trunk extend straight up through the head or does it divide into branches? Are there many small branches or few large branches?

4. Is the bark of tree rough, smooth, scaly, or is it divided by fissures?

5. Do the fissures extend up and down or crosswise or in both directions? Are the ridges between the fissures sharp, rounded, or flattened? How many inches across the ridge from the bottom of the fissure on each side?

6. Are the surface layers of the bark stiff or flexible? Are they fast to the tree or easily peeled off? Are they shed in stripes or in bits?

7. Is the color of the bark white, gray, dark gray, blackish, blotched, yellowish-brown, reddish-brown, or dark brown?

8. Are the leaves placed alternate or opposite on the twigs? Is the leaf simple or compound?

9. Is the leaf polished, smooth, dull, rough, or hairy on the upper side? Compare the upper and undersides in color and texture.

10. Sketch or trace the leaf showing the stem, the petiole, and the veins, and be especially careful to draw the edges accurately.

11. When does the tree blossom?

Are the flowers perfect or are those that bear pollen separate from those that develop the fruit? If so, are they on the same tree or on different trees?

12. Describe or sketch the blossoms of the tree.

13. When is the fruit ripe? Describe it or sketch it and tell how it is carried from the parent tree so that the seeds may find a place to grow.

Consult the manuals of forestry and tree books and give an account of every thing that is of interest concerning this tree, including its native place, its history and its uses by man; and any quotations from literature ---- especially poetry that may have been written concerning this species.

Date ....

Name of tree ....

1. Where is it growing? Hillside, near stream, swamp, mountain, valley, open field, along fences, in the forest, along the edge of the forest

2. If growing in the open, indicate its general shape thus: Select one of the following outlines most closely resembling the tree with the pencil and add the trunk showing its proportion to the head of the tree and draw in the larger branches, changing the outline to represent the tree.

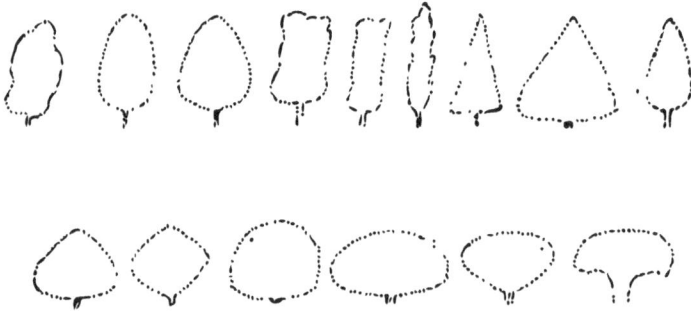

3. Does the bole or trunk extend straight up through the head or does it divide into branches? Are there many small branches or few large branches?

4. Is the bark of tree rough, smooth, scaly, or is it divided by fissures?

5. Do the fissures extend up and down or crosswise or in both directions? Are the ridges between the fissures sharp, rounded, or flattened? How many inches across the ridge from the bottom of the fissure on each side?

6. Are the surface layers of the bark stiff or flexible? Are they fast to the tree or easily peeled off? Are they shed in stripes or in bits?

7. Is the color of the bark white, gray, dark gray, blackish, blotched, yellowish-brown, reddish-brown, or dark brown?

8. Are the leaves placed alternate or opposite on the twigs? Is the leaf simple or compound?

9. Is the leaf polished, smooth, dull, rough, or hairy on the upper side? Compare the upper and undersides in color and texture.

10. Sketch or trace the leaf showing the stem, the petiole, and the veins, and be especially careful to draw the edges accurately.

11. When does the tree blossom?

Are the flowers perfect or are those that bear pollen separate from those that develop the fruit? If so, are they on the same tree or on different trees?

12. Describe or sketch the blossoms of the tree.

13. When is the fruit ripe? Describe it or sketch it and tell how it is carried from the parent tree so that the seeds may find a place to grow.

Consult the manuals of forestry and tree books and give an account of every thing that is of interest concerning this tree, including its native place, its history and its uses by man; and any quotations from literature ---- especially poetry that may have been written concerning this species.

Date ....

Name of tree ....

1. Where is it growing? Hillside, near stream, swamp, mountain, valley, open field, along fences, in the forest, along the edge of the forest

2. If growing in the open, indicate its general shape thus: Select one of the following outlines most closely resembling the tree with the pencil and add the trunk showing its proportion to the head of the tree and draw in the larger branches, changing the outline to represent the tree.

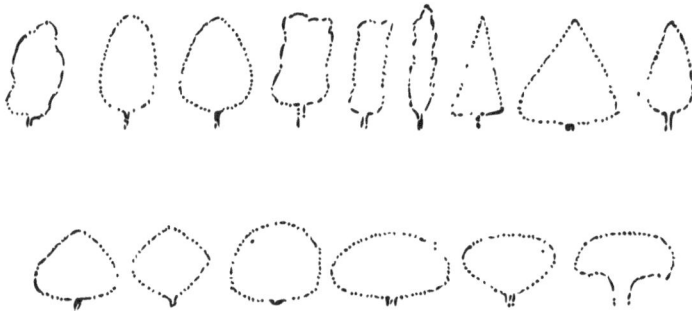

3. Does the bole or trunk extend straight up through the head or does it divide into branches? Are there many small branches or few large branches?

4. Is the bark of tree rough, smooth, scaly, or is it divided by fissures?

5. Do the fissures extend up and down or crosswise or in both directions? Are the ridges between the fissures sharp, rounded, or flattened? How many inches across the ridge from the bottom of the fissure on each side?

6. Are the surface layers of the bark stiff or flexible? Are they fast to the tree or easily peeled off? Are they shed in stripes or in bits?

7. Is the color of the bark white, gray, dark gray, blackish, blotched, yellowish-brown, reddish-brown, or dark brown?

8. Are the leaves placed alternate or opposite on the twigs? Is the leaf simple or compound?

9. Is the leaf polished, smooth, dull, rough, or hairy on the upper side? Compare the upper and undersides in color and texture.

10. Sketch or trace the leaf showing the stem, the petiole, and the veins, and be especially careful to draw the edges accurately.

11. When does the tree blossom?

   Are the flowers perfect or are those that bear pollen separate from those that develop the fruit? If so, are they on the same tree or on different trees?

12. Describe or sketch the blossoms of the tree.

13. When is the fruit ripe? Describe it or sketch it and tell how it is carried from the parent tree so that the seeds may find a place to grow.

Consult the manuals of forestry and tree books and give an account of every thing that is of interest concerning this tree, including its native place, its history and its uses by man; and any quotations from literature ---- especially poetry that may have been written concerning this species.

Date ....

Name of tree ....

1. Where is it growing? Hillside, near stream, swamp, mountain, valley, open field, along fences, in the forest, along the edge of the forest

2. If growing in the open, indicate its general shape thus: Select one of the following outlines most closely resembling the tree with the pencil and add the trunk showing its proportion to the head of the tree and draw in the larger branches, changing the outline to represent the tree.

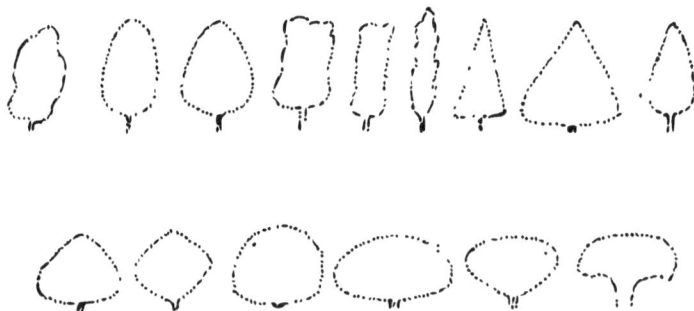

3. Does the bole or trunk extend straight up through the head or does it divide into branches? Are there many small branches or few large branches?

4. Is the bark of tree rough, smooth, scaly, or is it divided by fissures?

5. Do the fissures extend up and down or crosswise or in both directions? Are the ridges between the fissures sharp, rounded, or flattened? How many inches across the ridge from the bottom of the fissure on each side?

6. Are the surface layers of the bark stiff or flexible? Are they fast to the tree or easily peeled off? Are they shed in stripes or in bits?

7. Is the color of the bark white, gray, dark gray, blackish, blotched, yellowish-brown, reddish-brown, or dark brown?

8. Are the leaves placed alternate or opposite on the twigs? Is the leaf simple or compound?

9. Is the leaf polished, smooth, dull, rough, or hairy on the upper side? Compare the upper and undersides in color and texture.

10. Sketch or trace the leaf showing the stem, the petiole, and the veins, and be especially careful to draw the edges accurately.

11. When does the tree blossom?

Are the flowers perfect or are those that bear pollen separate from those that develop the fruit? If so, are they on the same tree or on different trees?

12. Describe or sketch the blossoms of the tree.

13. When is the fruit ripe? Describe it or sketch it and tell how it is carried from the parent tree so that the seeds may find a place to grow.

Consult the manuals of forestry and tree books and give an account of every thing that is of interest concerning this tree, including its native place, its history and its uses by man; and any quotations from literature ---- especially poetry that may have been written concerning this species.

Date ....

Name of tree ....

1. Where is it growing? Hillside, near stream, swamp, mountain, valley, open field, along fences, in the forest, along the edge of the forest

2. If growing in the open, indicate its general shape thus: Select one of the following outlines most closely resembling the tree with the pencil and add the trunk showing its proportion to the head of the tree and draw in the larger branches, changing the outline to represent the tree.

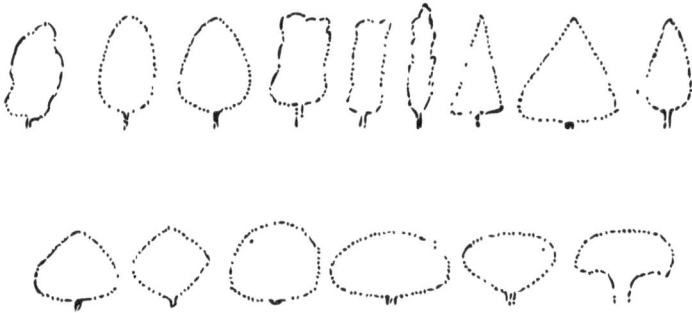

3. Does the bole or trunk extend straight up through the head or does it divide into branches? Are there many small branches or few large branches?

4. Is the bark of tree rough, smooth, scaly, or is it divided by fissures?

5. Do the fissures extend up and down or crosswise or in both directions? Are the ridges between the fissures sharp, rounded, or flattened? How many inches across the ridge from the bottom of the fissure on each side?

6. Are the surface layers of the bark stiff or flexible? Are they fast to the tree or easily peeled off? Are they shed in stripes or in bits?

7. Is the color of the bark white, gray, dark gray, blackish, blotched, yellowish-brown, reddish-brown, or dark brown?

8. Are the leaves placed alternate or opposite on the twigs? Is the leaf simple or compound?

9. Is the leaf polished, smooth, dull, rough, or hairy on the upper side? Compare the upper and undersides in color and texture.

10. Sketch or trace the leaf showing the stem, the petiole, and the veins, and be especially careful to draw the edges accurately.

11. When does the tree blossom?

Are the flowers perfect or are those that bear pollen separate from those that develop the fruit? If so, are they on the same tree or on different trees?

12. Describe or sketch the blossoms of the tree.

13. When is the fruit ripe? Describe it or sketch it and tell how it is carried from the parent tree so that the seeds may find a place to grow.

Consult the manuals of forestry and tree books and give an account of every thing that is of interest concerning this tree, including its native place, its history and its uses by man; and any quotations from literature ---- especially poetry that may have been written concerning this species.

UNDERSCORE THE WORDS WHICH DESCRIBE THE TREE

Date ....

Name of tree ....

1. Where is it growing? Hillside, near stream, swamp, mountain, valley, open field, along fences, in the forest, along the edge of the forest

2. If growing in the open, indicate its general shape thus: Select one of the following outlines most closely resembling the tree with the pencil and add the trunk showing its proportion to the head of the tree and draw in the larger branches, changing the outline to represent the tree.

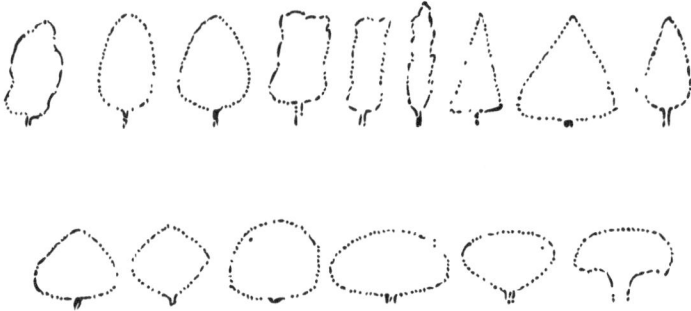

3. Does the bole or trunk extend straight up through the head or does it divide into branches? Are there many small branches or few large branches?

4. Is the bark of tree rough, smooth, scaly, or is it divided by fissures?

5. Do the fissures extend up and down or crosswise or in both directions? Are the ridges between the fissures sharp, rounded, or flattened? How many inches across the ridge from the bottom of the fissure on each side?

6. Are the surface layers of the bark stiff or flexible? Are they fast to the tree or easily peeled off? Are they shed in stripes or in bits?

7. Is the color of the bark white, gray, dark gray, blackish, blotched, yellowish-brown, reddish-brown, or dark brown?

8. Are the leaves placed alternate or opposite on the twigs? Is the leaf simple or compound?

9. Is the leaf polished, smooth, dull, rough, or hairy on the upper side? Compare the upper and undersides in color and texture.

10. Sketch or trace the leaf showing the stem, the petiole, and the veins, and be especially careful to draw the edges accurately.

11. When does the tree blossom?

Are the flowers perfect or are those that bear pollen separate from those that develop the fruit? If so, are they on the same tree or on different trees?

12. Describe or sketch the blossoms of the tree.

13. When is the fruit ripe? Describe it or sketch it and tell how it is carried from the parent tree so that the seeds may find a place to grow.

Consult the manuals of forestry and tree books and give an account of every thing that is of interest concerning this tree, including its native place, its history and its uses by man; and any quotations from literature ---- especially poetry that may have been written concerning this species.

Date ....

Name of tree ....

1. Where is it growing? Hillside, near stream, swamp, mountain, valley, open field, along fences, in the forest, along the edge of the forest

2. If growing in the open, indicate its general shape thus: Select one of the following outlines most closely resembling the tree with the pencil and add the trunk showing its proportion to the head of the tree and draw in the larger branches, changing the outline to represent the tree.

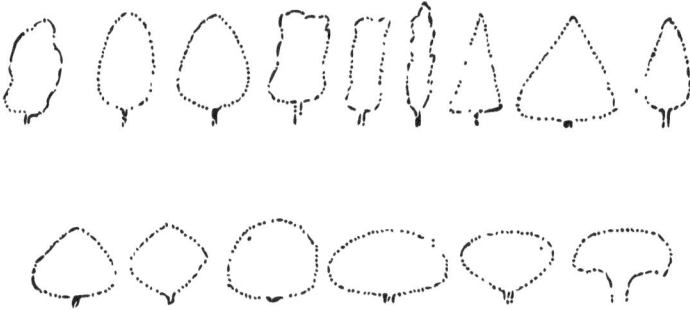

3. Does the bole or trunk extend straight up through the head or does it divide into branches? Are there many small branches or few large branches?

4. Is the bark of tree rough, smooth, scaly, or is it divided by fissures?

5. Do the fissures extend up and down or crosswise or in both directions? Are the ridges between the fissures sharp, rounded, or flattened? How many inches across the ridge from the bottom of the fissure on each side?

6. Are the surface layers of the bark stiff or flexible? Are they fast to the tree or easily peeled off? Are they shed in stripes or in bits?

7. Is the color of the bark white, gray, dark gray, blackish, blotched, yellowish-brown, reddish-brown, or dark brown?

8. Are the leaves placed alternate or opposite on the twigs? Is the leaf simple or compound?

9. Is the leaf polished, smooth, dull, rough, or hairy on the upper side? Compare the upper and undersides in color and texture.

10. Sketch or trace the leaf showing the stem, the petiole, and the veins, and be especially careful to draw the edges accurately.

11. When does the tree blossom?

Are the flowers perfect or are those that bear pollen separate from those that develop the fruit? If so, are they on the same tree or on different trees?

12. Describe or sketch the blossoms of the tree.

13. When is the fruit ripe? Describe it or sketch it and tell how it is carried from the parent tree so that the seeds may find a place to grow.

Consult the manuals of forestry and tree books and give an account of every thing that is of interest concerning this tree, including its native place, its history and its uses by man; and any quotations from literature ---- especially poetry that may have been written concerning this species.

Date ....

Name of tree ....

1. Where is it growing? Hillside, near stream, swamp, mountain, valley, open field, along fences, in the forest, along the edge of the forest

2. If growing in the open, indicate its general shape thus: Select one of the following outlines most closely resembling the tree with the pencil and add the trunk showing its proportion to the head of the tree and draw in the larger branches, changing the outline to represent the tree.

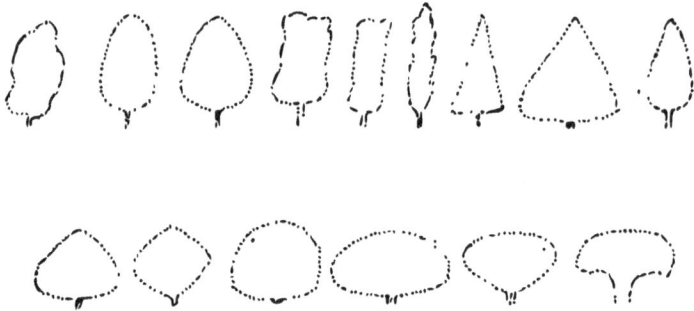

3. Does the bole or trunk extend straight up through the head or does it divide into branches? Are there many small branches or few large branches?

4. Is the bark of tree rough, smooth, scaly, or is it divided by fissures?

5. Do the fissures extend up and down or crosswise or in both directions? Are the ridges between the fissures sharp, rounded, or flattened? How many inches across the ridge from the bottom of the fissure on each side?

6. Are the surface layers of the bark stiff or flexible? Are they fast to the tree or easily peeled off? Are they shed in stripes or in bits?

7. Is the color of the bark white, gray, dark gray, blackish, blotched, yellowish-brown, reddish-brown, or dark brown?

8. Are the leaves placed alternate or opposite on the twigs? Is the leaf simple or compound?

9. Is the leaf polished, smooth, dull, rough, or hairy on the upper side? Compare the upper and undersides in color and texture.

10. Sketch or trace the leaf showing the stem, the petiole, and the veins, and be especially careful to draw the edges accurately.

11. When does the tree blossom?

Are the flowers perfect or are those that bear pollen separate from those that develop the fruit? If so, are they on the same tree or on different trees?

12. Describe or sketch the blossoms of the tree.

13. When is the fruit ripe? Describe it or sketch it and tell how it is carried from the parent tree so that the seeds may find a place to grow.

Consult the manuals of forestry and tree books and give an account of every thing that is of interest concerning this tree, including its native place, its history and its uses by man; and any quotations from literature ---- especially poetry that may have been written concerning this species.

Cone-Bearing Trees

THE EVERGREENS

Determine the kind of tree by the following table:

PINES

- Foliage needle-like
- Leaves arranged in bundles or tufts.
- Leaves arranged in bundles of two to six with a sheath at base.

aa. Many leaves arranged in tufts without sheaths at base and shed in winter.

LARCHES

bb. Leaves set singly and scattered along the branch.

FIRS

c. Leaves flat, blunt at tip, pale beneath and two-ranked on twig, cones standing erect.

HEMLOCKS

cc. Cones drooping and the leaves with little stalks.

ccc. Leaves four-sided in cross section, sharp at tip, not pale beneath.

SPRUCES

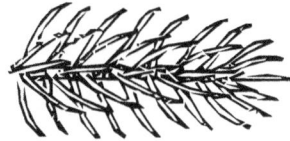

aa. Foliage scale-like or spiny.

WHITE CEDAR
OR
ARBORVITAE

b. Foliage scale-like small, close pressed to the twig, fruit very small cone.

JUNIPER OR
RED CEDAR

bb. Foliage spiny or scale-like or both, fruit a blue berry.

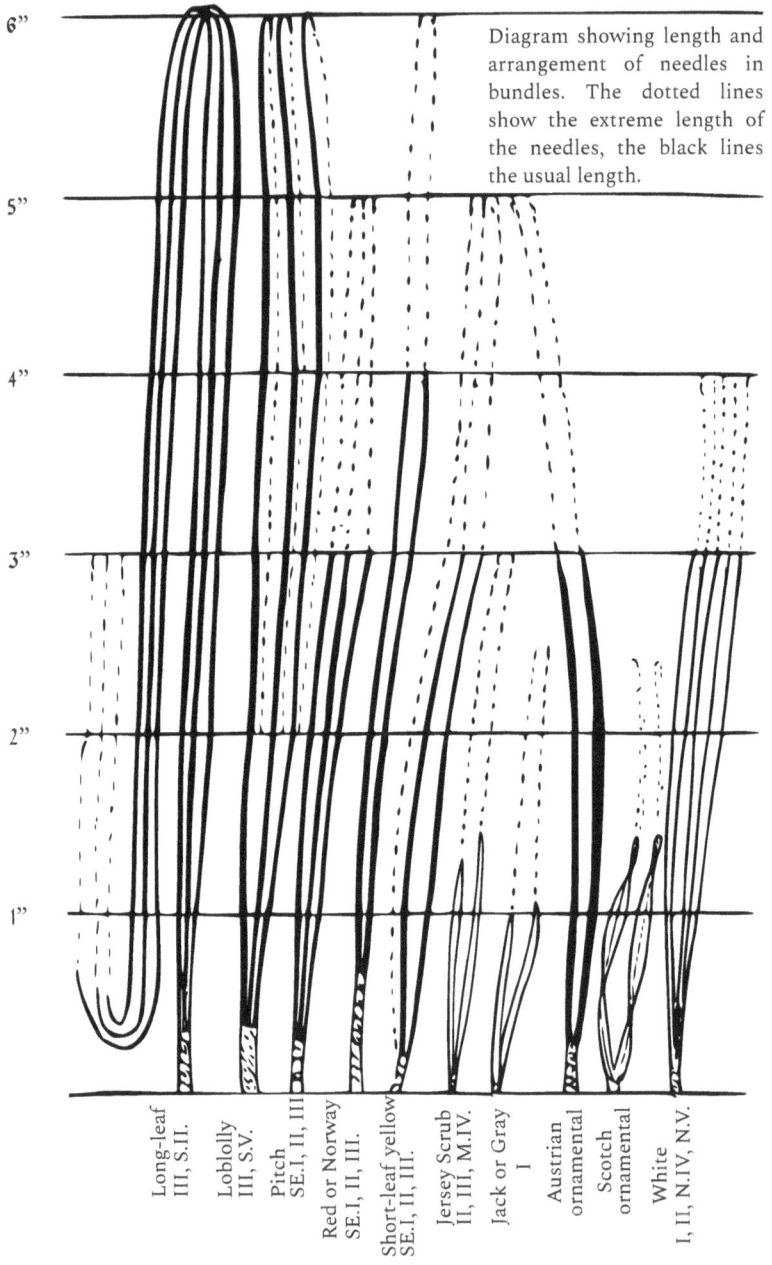

Diagram showing length and arrangement of needles in bundles. The dotted lines show the extreme length of the needles, the black lines the usual length.

Long-leaf
III, S.II.

Loblolly
III, S.V.

Pitch
SE.I, II, III

Red or Norway
SE.I, II, III.

Short-leaf yellow
SE.I, II, III.

Jersey Scrub
II, III, M.IV.

Jack or Gray
I

Austrian
ornamental

Scotch
ornamental

White
I, II, N.IV, N.V.

120

STUDY OF A CONE-BEARING TREE

Name of species ....

1. In what locality is the tree growing? Hillside, near stream, swamp, mountain, valley, open field, along fences, in the forest, along the edge of the forest.

2. If growing in the open, what is its general shape? Estimate the height of the tree and the thickness of the bole.

3. How far from the ground do the first branches come off?

4. Does the bole or trunk extend straight up through the head or does it divide into branches?

5. Is the bark of the tree rough or smooth, scaly or divided by noticeable fissures? What is the color?

6. Are the fissures in the bark vertical or crosswise? Are the ridges between the fissures sharp or flattened? How many inches across the ridge from the base of the fissure on each side?

7. Sketch the leaves or needles showing how they are arranged on the twig. If a pine, show how many needles in a bundle.

8. Study a single needle or leaf. How long is it? Is it straight or curved? Flexible or stiff? Cut it across and examine with a lens and describe or sketch its shape.

9. Study the cone. Does it grow near the tip, at the tip, or along the sides of the branch? Does it hang down or stand out stiffly? Describe its general shape and size or sketch it.

10. Take a single scale of the cone and describe or sketch it. Has the scale a thickened tip? Has it a spine near the tip?

11. Where in the cone are the seeds? Describe or sketch a seed.

12. In Spring, study the blossoms. Where on the branches are the young cones? Are the cones upright or drooping at this stage? Describe the catkins that bear the pollen? How long is each? How many grouped together? Where on the twigs are they borne?

13. General remarks upon this tree:

Consult the manuals of forestry and tree books and give an account of every thing that is of interest concerning this tree, including its native place, its history and its uses by man; and any quotations from literature ---- especially poetry that may have been written concerning this species.

STUDY OF A CONE-BEARING TREE

Name of species ....

1. In what locality is the tree growing? Hillside, near stream, swamp, mountain, valley, open field, along fences, in the forest, along the edge of the forest.

2. If growing in the open, what is its general shape? Estimate the height of the tree and the thickness of the bole.

3. How far from the ground do the first branches come off?

4. Does the bole or trunk extend straight up through the head or does it divide into branches?

5. Is the bark of the tree rough or smooth, scaly or divided by noticeable fissures? What is the color?

6. Are the fissures in the bark vertical or crosswise? Are the ridges between the fissures sharp or flattened? How many inches across the ridge from the base of the fissure on each side?

7. Sketch the leaves or needles showing how they are arranged on the twig. If a pine, show how many needles in a bundle.

8. Study a single needle or leaf. How long is it? Is it straight or curved? Flexible or stiff? Cut it across and examine with a lens and describe or sketch its shape.

9. Study the cone. Does it grow near the tip, at the tip, or along the sides of the branch? Does it hang down or stand out stiffly? Describe its general shape and size or sketch it.

10. Take a single scale of the cone and describe or sketch it. Has the scale a thickened tip? Has it a spine near the tip?

11. Where in the cone are the seeds? Describe or sketch a seed.

12. In Spring, study the blossoms. Where on the branches are the young cones? Are the cones upright or drooping at this stage? Describe the catkins that bear the pollen? How long is each? How many grouped together? Where on the twigs are they borne?

13. General remarks upon this tree:

Consult the manuals of forestry and tree books and give an account of every thing that is of interest concerning this tree, including its native place, its history and its uses by man; and any quotations from literature ---- especially poetry that may have been written concerning this species.

Name of species ....

1. In what locality is the tree growing? Hillside, near stream, swamp, mountain, valley, open field, along fences, in the forest, along the edge of the forest.

2. If growing in the open, what is its general shape? Estimate the height of the tree and the thickness of the bole.

3. How far from the ground do the first branches come off?

4. Does the bole or trunk extend straight up through the head or does it divide into branches?

5. Is the bark of the tree rough or smooth, scaly or divided by noticeable fissures? What is the color?

6. Are the fissures in the bark vertical or crosswise? Are the ridges between the fissures sharp or flattened? How many inches across the ridge from the base of the fissure on each side?

7. Sketch the leaves or needles showing how they are arranged on the twig. If a pine, show how many needles in a bundle.

8. Study a single needle or leaf. How long is it? Is it straight or curved? Flexible or stiff? Cut it across and examine with a lens and describe or sketch its shape.

9. Study the cone. Does it grow near the tip, at the tip, or along the sides of the branch? Does it hang down or stand out stiffly? Describe its general shape and size or sketch it.

10. Take a single scale of the cone and describe or sketch it. Has the scale a thickened tip? Has it a spine near the tip?

130

11. Where in the cone are the seeds? Describe or sketch a seed.

12. In Spring, study the blossoms. Where on the branches are the young cones? Are the cones upright or drooping at this stage? Describe the catkins that bear the pollen? How long is each? How many grouped together? Where on the twigs are they borne?

13. General remarks upon this tree:

Consult the manuals of forestry and tree books and give an account of every thing that is of interest concerning this tree, including its native place, its history and its uses by man; and any quotations from literature ---- especially poetry that may have been written concerning this species.

STUDY OF A CONE-BEARING TREE

Name of species ....

1. In what locality is the tree growing? Hillside, near stream, swamp, mountain, valley, open field, along fences, in the forest, along the edge of the forest.

2. If growing in the open, what is its general shape? Estimate the height of the tree and the thickness of the bole.

3. How far from the ground do the first branches come off?

4. Does the bole or trunk extend straight up through the head or does it divide into branches?

5. Is the bark of the tree rough or smooth, scaly or divided by noticeable fissures? What is the color?

6. Are the fissures in the bark vertical or crosswise? Are the ridges between the fissures sharp or flattened? How many inches across the ridge from the base of the fissure on each side?

7. Sketch the leaves or needles showing how they are arranged on the twig. If a pine, show how many needles in a bundle.

8. Study a single needle or leaf. How long is it? Is it straight or curved? Flexible or stiff? Cut it across and examine with a lens and describe or sketch its shape.

9. Study the cone. Does it grow near the tip, at the tip, or along the sides of the branch? Does it hang down or stand out stiffly? Describe its general shape and size or sketch it.

10. Take a single scale of the cone and describe or sketch it. Has the scale a thickened tip? Has it a spine near the tip?

11. Where in the cone are the seeds? Describe or sketch a seed.

12. In Spring, study the blossoms. Where on the branches are the young cones? Are the cones upright or drooping at this stage? Describe the catkins that bear the pollen? How long is each? How many grouped together? Where on the twigs are they borne?

13. General remarks upon this tree:

Consult the manuals of forestry and tree books and give an account of every thing that is of interest concerning this tree, including its native place, its history and its uses by man; and any quotations from literature ---- especially poetry that may have been written concerning this species.

STUDY OF A CONE-BEARING TREE

Name of species ....

1. In what locality is the tree growing? Hillside, near stream, swamp, mountain, valley, open field, along fences, in the forest, along the edge of the forest.

2. If growing in the open, what is its general shape? Estimate the height of the tree and the thickness of the bole.

3. How far from the ground do the first branches come off?

4. Does the bole or trunk extend straight up through the head or does it divide into branches?

5. Is the bark of the tree rough or smooth, scaly or divided by noticeable fissures? What is the color?

6. Are the fissures in the bark vertical or crosswise? Are the ridges between the fissures sharp or flattened? How many inches across the ridge from the base of the fissure on each side?

7. Sketch the leaves or needles showing how they are arranged on the twig. If a pine, show how many needles in a bundle.

8. Study a single needle or leaf. How long is it? Is it straight or curved? Flexible or stiff? Cut it across and examine with a lens and describe or sketch its shape.

9. Study the cone. Does it grow near the tip, at the tip, or along the sides of the branch? Does it hang down or stand out stiffly? Describe its general shape and size or sketch it.

10. Take a single scale of the cone and describe or sketch it. Has the scale a thickened tip? Has it a spine near the tip?

11. Where in the cone are the seeds? Describe or sketch a seed.

12. In Spring, study the blossoms. Where on the branches are the young cones? Are the cones upright or drooping at this stage? Describe the catkins that bear the pollen? How long is each? How many grouped together? Where on the twigs are they borne?

13. General remarks upon this tree:

Consult the manuals of forestry and tree books and give an account of every thing that is of interest concerning this tree, including its native place, its history and its uses by man; and any quotations from literature ---- especially poetry that may have been written concerning this species.

www.ingramcontent.com/pod-product-compliance
Lightning Source LLC
Chambersburg PA
CBHW032055040426
42335CB00037B/752